T0021383

I WAS IN HEAVEN

F.O. Owojori

authorHOUSE®

AuthorHouse™ UK Ltd.
500 Avebury Boulevard
Central Milton Keynes, MK9 2BE
www.authorhouse.co.uk
Phone: 08001974150

First published by AuthorHouse 6/28/2011

ISBN: 978-1-4567-8375-4 (sc)

Table of Contents

Preface

Heaven is real. Eternity is real.

The coming of the Lord is very near; different things that happen around us in several ways have shown to us that we are in the last days. We are in the last days and days that world becomes more difficult in readiness for the coming of the Lord Jesus Christ, just like a woman in travail. It takes the grace and mercies of God to be focused these days in readiness for the coming of the Lord.

Many children of God need unique encounters in their lives to help them set their hearts desires on the kingdom above. May He set your heart and gaze firmly on Jesus Christ. I pray that the Lord will sensitize the church leaders at this hour to preach and teach more on the kingdom of God, holiness and purity of lives and characters.

> **Matt 6:10 Thy kingdom come. Thy will be done in earth, as *it is* in heaven.**

It is my prayers that the Lord will set you with passion for readiness and help you to do whatever is necessary in readiness for the Kingdom of God cometh.

Dedication

Dedicated to the Lord Jesus who left the awesome glory and power, came to the earth for my salvation and redemption, not only for me but for the whole world that as many would believe in Him would have eternal life.

To Him are the glory, the honor, the power and the kingdom forever and ever. Amen.

To the saints I fellowshipped with in my experience of heaven who have greatly impacted and inspired me.

To my wife, Mary and my three wonderful daughters; Dasola, Ibukun, baby Zion. The Lord bless you all.

1Ti 1:12 and I thank Christ Jesus our Lord, who hath enabled me, for that he counted me faithful, putting me into the ministry;

Introduction

It has taken me several months to write this testimony and compile it to a book. Several times I have found it extremely difficult looking for the right word to use to describe my experience. It's been like I have shallow limitations in vocabularies and do not really possess the needed parameters to describe heaven and joy of the saints.

Beloved, you are indeed blessed to read this testimony after also several attacks from the enemy to prevent this testimony from being published. The enemy satan attacked the first computer used in typing and saving the manuscript and it crashed, the first CD used in saving the manuscript was unusually and strangely wiped away. Thank God for the victory He has brought in all these things. This testimony is divinely ordained to reach you and inspire you towards the kingdom of God. Amen.

Chapter 1
Heaven Is Real

It is my prayer that what you are about to read will bring reformation to your life, separate you from the love of this world and bring the kingdom of God to you. Amen.

Journey from Lagos, Nigeria to Benin, Nigeria.

I travelled on 9th June, 2009 in a luxurious bus from Lagos (southwestern Nigeria) to Aba (eastern part of Nigeria).The purpose of my journey was to carry out an official assignment with a client the next morning. Ordinarily I was meant to fly by plane that day but due to delays from account section of my company to issue out funds on time, and some other factors, all my favorite airlines had all been booked so it necessitated I had to travel by bus and considering the urgency and time of my appointment with client the next morning I had to travel by night, and it was a night time journey.

I have never travelled to eastern part of Nigeria by night journey before. The luxurious bus was full, with about 46 passengers and their luggage, we left Lagos around 8pm, the journey was really good until we were about to reach Benin city(Nigeria).Benin city is about 4 hours journey from Lagos(100km/hr).There were police checkpoints all along the route. Around 2am in the midnight just close to Benin City, armed robbers attacked and shot our vehicle, bullets have punctured the tyres so the driver was forced to park. The scare of the armed robbers made the driver run for his life, leaving the passengers to the mercies of the robbers. Some of the passengers too were able to run from the vehicle while some still sat down in the vehicle for fear.

Ordinary Flowers in Heaven Give Lights

I managed to be part of the folks that ran away from the vehicle, running some few meters from the bus, I fell down and that's all I remembered about the robbery attack. I had passed out. The next thing will shock you

I appeared in a place different to the incidence of the robbery attack. I was in a place whereby the flowers give lights like lamps. I appeared in heaven. Then I appeared before a big white house built like a castle surrounded by tall, leafy trees. What the Lord Jesus said about His father's house is true and confirmed

> **John 14:2 In my Father's house are many mansions: if *it were* not *so*, I would have told you. I go to prepare a place for you.**

There are mansions prepared. I entered the house, and I could see it was white inside too and yet again to my amazement, I met people with joyful faces and smiles and all dressed in blistering white short-sleeved garments, they all smiled at me as if they were expecting my arrival, and infact they had expected me, I have arrived into heaven's warmest reception and glory, their presence and their countenances were so fascinating, and all were radiating with sheer brightness of glory. I could feel the presence of the Lord everywhere.

All of the people were not people I have met before, but they greeted and welcomed me with such love, joyfulness and warmth that I would not forget for the rest of my life, they made me feel specially loved than I used to see. I knew they were saints based on the things they shared with me later on. Every human being who has gone through the earth should desire not to miss this place and experience.

One of the Saints Is a Protocol Officer.

One of the saints was leading me on to places inside the big house. He behaved like the Protocol officer or guide, slim built and about three inches taller than me, I am six feet tall. This saint is very friendly, full of life, enthusiasm and limitless energy .It might interest you to know I could describe and recognize semblance to this saint's voice even after I left heaven, I have met someone with resemblance to his voice. This saint was attached to me; he followed me wherever I went and also brought me to some places too. I would call this saint the protocol officer.

SUPERNATURAL KNOWLEDGE-I discovered I had supernatural knowledge just by sighting things. There was what I could describe as a flash light from me pointing to about three of the saints there, and I had the knowledge right there that they were people who rose from their tombs into heavens, and at that same time, the protocol officer that was leading me to get familiar with the house told me the same thing about the three people.

I looked at the three people and they all smiled back at me and their smiles revealed "oh we knew what you saw", immediately their tombs appeared before them in sporadic fashions so that I could see them and I saw their three white empty tombs. These three saints have already experienced resurrection. I saw from the scriptures that graves were opened when Jesus was crucified.

> **Mat 27:52 And the graves were opened; and many bodies of the saints which slept arose,**

I can just describe that these were like archives in heaven. One thing worthy of note was that I already felt at home there and it was like a fellowship with brethren and the spirit of togetherness, the harmony, the completeness had overwhelmed me-It is truly the presence of the lord.

It is truly the presence of saints-true cloud of witnesses. So after that, I moved on inside the apartment in heaven, then the saint that was leading me in the mansion to familiarize me spoke with such enthusiasms and friendliness like we have been friends for a very long time, this saint had impacted me with heavenly flair and tremendous heavenly joy, I have later found out.

We Saw the Earth from Heaven

I moved to another saint to say hello for he smiled at me and he moved his hand like stretching it forward and coincidentally he knew there was lying-in-state ceremony for him on earth and he opened it for all to see and all the saints in that apartment in the big house could see and saw there was a lying-in-state been conducted for him on earth, and it was shown ,and all the saints saw what they were doing on earth from heaven, and I saw from heaven very clearly the ceremony on earth, and the views were like the bird's viewpoint and human's viewpoint. This saint made me see that he was a new entrant into the house and he had died on earth not quite long.

I could see that the lying-in-state ceremony was being conducted in a temperate region (for it was cold there even during the day), then I noticed the man was an aged fat man on earth, covered with mixed red and white colored blanket, laid down like a man who sleeps, placed outside the house, but to my surprise he looks so smart, slim, young and refreshed. In heaven, there is God's beauty that transcends what we see on earth

Then, it was like the man whose lying in state was getting done on earth was tired watching and everybody too and we all switched to something else. It's like saints in heavens do not really appreciate all the ceremonies, and it has given me the feeling that heaven does not enjoy our earthly frivolities sometimes.

The Armed Robbers Have Gone and Other Passengers Couldn't Find Me

All this while, the armed robbers on earth had gone, and the passengers that ran out of the bus had returned, and it remained just one of the passengers-and the passenger was me, they searched all around the bus, the nearby bush for over six hours and could not find me. Then they thought maybe I ran away during the attack, they thought about continuing the journey in the night without me but one lady would not consent in the bus, she was the lady that sat beside me in the vehicle.

She was going to owerri (Nigeria), while I had my destination for Aba (Nigeria).The lady out of shock and disbelief that a matured man like me would miss out of all the passengers, had insisted my luggage be searched, and they found over 200,000 naira (about USD1, 500) and my laptop computer, so they convinced themselves that I wouldn't have gone away without coming back for my belongings. So, all the men in the bus got out and conducted a search looking for me again, they did all these, yet could not locate where I was.

And the search continued till daybreak.

Chapter 2
Seven Hours of Search, God Hid Me

The search was intensified. They searched the scenes of the robbery incidence for over six hours and they could not locate me. How do I explain that I was lying down lifeless some few meters away from the bus and they could not find me for that long?. God hid me and blindfolded them by His divine presence. I can't explain this. I have gone through the scriptures to try and see if there's a way I could explain this but I will say it was done so that the purpose of God might be achieved.

My mobile phone number was collected from my wife (my wife's number was on the manifest as my next of kin) and around 8.45 am in the morning. They, together with my wife have dialed my mobile phone with no responses from me for some time, the calls to my phone was intensified.

Persistent calls and I was near the bus lying down, yet they could not hear the ringing of the phone, later on the passengers heard my phone ringing and found me very near the bus, after the several hours of search, I can only call this a 'wonder and divine'. "So near yet so far away".

My body was very weak, they gave me water to drink, thought I had bites, was rushed to the hospital for treatment in Benin City. All this time, my earthly memory was just returning and later on I really felt I am in a strange place-the world, I felt it so deep that I was longing for the saints again. The feeling was likened to 'been deported' from a promisingly beautiful country to a harsh, unloving nation. I felt lost and strange in the world. The atmosphere in the world was not pleasant.

Then, my spirit has just arrived back to the earth and when they saw me, the very first thing I asked them was; what's happening here? I said it very harshly. I have forgotten about the armed robbery incidence. To me it was like I did not understand why they were troubled? It was like I had fallen down for about 2 minutes and woke up, but indeed it was 7-hour search.

Please take note that about the same time, prior to the passengers locating me, the saints in heaven have already told me it was time to go back as you would read in subsequent chapters.

Now after about six weeks. I later asked the Lord why He didn't allow the passengers to see me throughout the hours until I returned. The Lord made me understood, if they had seen me, they would have spread wrong messages, so He had to disallow them from seeing me. I assumed if they saw me they might call on the mortuary for attention, I also imagined how my wife would feel or react, if she heard that her husband was dead. Since it was God's purpose, He didn't let them see me and He refused them leave

I knew I had missed some wonderful people. then I had very clear feelings of rejection for the world, felt so lonely at first, later the Holy Spirit took away the loneliness and ministered to me, and I had found clearer settings in my spirit, coupled with a renewed sense of urgency for dedication towards the course of the kingdom, to tell men and women about this experience that the Kingdom is our place and we must always ponder in our hearts about this, and we must regularly seek for the Kingdom. I just wanted to go all out and fulfill the ministry. I pray there shall be a consistent, systematic and pragmatic approach from the church (the body of Christ) to let believers know this and re-ignite their passions for the love of God's Kingdom. I pray that the Lord will minister to you.

> **15 Love not the world, neither the things that are in the world. If any man love the world, the love of the Father is not in him. 16 For all that is in the world, the lust of the flesh, and the lust of the eyes, and the pride of life, is not of the Father, but is of the world. 17 And the world passeth away, and the lust thereof: but he that doeth the will of God abideth for ever.1 John 2:15**

Prayer1.Ask the Lord to help you to love Him, redirect your attention and love for this world and place them on the Kingdom.

2. Ask the Lord to help you to continually put your gaze on Jesus Christ and the kingdom.

3. Ask the Lord for zeal, passion for His kingdom. Very critical in these last days.

I am praying that the Church will come to maturity and understand our position as believers and saints on earth, that our attention would be on people's lives getting transformed, living holy, and set apart as vessels for God's use, that the church of Jesus would be in holiness, without blemish, spot or wrinkles as His coming is imminent.

Fellowship with the Saints

> Therefore, since we are surrounded by
> such a great cloud of witnesses, we must
> get rid of every weight and the sin that
> clings so closely, and run with endurance
> the race set out for us, keeping our eyes
> fixed on Jesus, the pioneer and perfecter
> of our faith. For the joy set out for him he
> endured the cross, disregarding its shame,
> and *has taken his seat at the right hand of
> the throne* of God. HEB 12:1-2

Beloved, during my visit to heaven I observed saints in heaven are actually interested and know about our walk with the Lord, there were things the saints told me about my personal calling and ministry; I could see they had the details about me. Through this, I am able to know that the saints see us as we run our race on earth. In the above scripture, the cloud of witnesses are the saints in heaven, who are just like supporters to athletes(similar to what goes on during race events).The saints are like supporting us, hurrying us up to finish the race in good time and faithfully. I have noticed that athletes don't wear heavy clothings or carry any material except the track suit, so as to be able to run effectively. In our journey with the lord, we must run to finish the race and in good time. Anything that could slow us down should be dropped.

Now weights may not necessarily be sins, but eventually it makes committing sins become easier. Weights are the kind of things that gradually become bridge to sins. If you allow the Lord to deal with you, you would be wise to let him help you with those things you feel do not matter or affect you in the race or those things you feel you can handle with your sensual and carnal wisdoms but they infact are weights and slow us down in the journey.

Sin that clings so closely-are those sins associated with our weaknesses before salvation and sins you have taken note as hindrance to your walk with God or weaknesses you always struggle with. The enemy could still use memories of those past sins to hunt us, and therefore they are sins that cling so closely. Some believers still struggle with some certain weaknesses and sins, and these have prevented them from running the race effectively, except you repent, those weaknesses could slow you, then stop you and eventually make you lose out in the race of the kingdom of heaven.

The Lord has made me realized that sins are beyond what we read from Gal 5:19,anything that breaks your communion with the Holy Ghost is sinful. The Lord will let you realize the victory over sin if you walk with Him

Run with endurance-Have you ever watched distance runners compete?. You will notice that the winners have certain qualities more than the loosers. The winners are always dogged, tenacious, determined, courageous, enduring (during hardship or tribulation)

Our journey in the spirit is a race, and we must be fit and abandon any weights that could slow us down or made us abandon the journey.

Prayer; Ask the Lord to help you in the race, by removing every entanglements, closely related sins, ungodly habits and attitudes, fleshly and carnal lusts that would be hindrance to you in your walk with the lord and in the race.

The race has to be run with endurance.

Dictionary meaning of endurance-the ability to withstand hardship or adversity ; *especially*: the ability to sustain a prolonged stressful effort or activity.

The Christian race is not easy as we need help from the Lord from time to time.

Believers have to set their gaze on Jesus firmly, and should not lose focus, there would be many things that would want to distract us, weaken us, get us carried away by the handiwork of satan, but our determination combined with our attention on Jesus Christ would save us.

How Can We Keep Our Attention on Jesus?

1. Allow the Kingdom of God to take first place in everything you do.
You must live for the kingdom of God.

> **1Th 2:12 That ye would walk worthy of God, who hath called you unto his kingdom and glory.**
>
> **And now the prize awaits me—the crown of righteousness that the Lord, the righteous Judge, will give me on that great day of his return. And the prize is not just for me but for all who eagerly look forward to his glorious return. 2timothy 4:8**

2. Live a holy life.
Having therefore these promises, dearly beloved, let us cleanse ourselves from all filthiness of the flesh and spirit, perfecting holiness in the fear of God.2 Cor 7:1

> **Follow peace with all men, and holiness, without which no man shall see the Lord. Heb 12:14**

3. A life crucified with Christ
Those who belong to Christ Jesus have nailed the passions

and desires of their sinful nature to his cross and crucified them there.

> **Gal 5:24 And they that are Christ's have crucified the flesh with the affections and lusts.**

> **Gal 5:25 If we live in the Spirit, let us also walk in the Spirit.**

Joy Undescribable in Heaven

I can't describe it. No perfect word here on earth to describe it. I have been searching for the closest word for description. It's difficult.

Chapter 3
What Happens When Believers Die?
(From White Tomb to White Throne)

And now, brothers and sisters, I want you to know what will happen to the Christians who have died so you will not be full of sorrow like people who have no hope.

> **14 For since we believe that Jesus died and was raised to life again, we also believe that when Jesus comes, God will bring back with Jesus all the Christians who have died.1 Thessalonians 4:13**

There is hope for a believer who dies in the Lord; there is everlasting pleasure and peace. If you are a believer in the Lord then rejoice there is eternity for you. I f you have anyone who dies as a sincere believer, you can rejoice.

Other believer can rejoice if one of them dies, for they shall surely fellowship with him/her again. Please read what revelation said about expectations for saints who departed the earth

> **4 And God shall wipe away all tears from their eyes; and there shall be no more**

> **death, neither sorrow, nor crying, neither shall there be any more pain: for the former things are passed away. Revelation 21:4**

Beloved, heaven culminates in an electrifying perfection of joy and sheer beauty of the lord. What a place for the believers, you should not miss it. Please, let me tell you further about my experience.

I Didn't Want to Come to the Earth Again.

During my visit to heaven, I had actually forgotten everything about the earth, wife, kids, families, job, things I use to remember with fondness. I have really enjoyed the fellowship of saints in heaven, the saints actually treated me as one of them, the love, the joy of seeing me, and the beautiful presence of the lord I felt made me forget about the earth. I cannot forget this experience throughout my entire life. I still crave for the experience I had while with the heavenly saints. It's really better to be in heaven than earth.

I was in heaven, the saints shared with me I have an earthly ministry and I remembered I moved away when I heard that, I did not want to come to the earth again, I had to be informed about three times about my earthly ministry and the fact that someone is looking for me(I later understood my wife has really tearfully disturbed God in prayers during the time my spirit was away, asking God to intervene).Infact when my spirit returned back to earth I had lost some of my earthly memory, it took me time to remember some other details I used to know.

Readers, eternity is real, and I can tell you if you are a believer and you die, the Lord has arrangement for you for your eternity but am afraid if you have not yet given your life to Jesus Christ, because hell is real for those who refuse Jesus into their lives. But I hope you would like to be in heaven for eternity. Then pray this prayer with faith.

Prayer-

Dear Lord, I know am a sinner (confess your known sins and ask the lord to forgive and cleanse you by the blood of Jesus).I believe and confess Jesus Christ as my Lord and Saviour. I accept Jesus Christ in to my life. Lord Jesus, please rule in my life from this moment in Jesus name. Lord Jesus, please help me not to return back to my former ways in Jesus name.

Reader, if you have done that, this simple prayer personally welcomes you into the kingdom of the Lord. Please take note of today's date (you can write it down) for it is the turning point of your life. I encourage you to share your testimony with me or find a sound gospel church to join, please let the overseer know about your newfound faith so that they may encourage you to grow in the lord. God bless you. You are now a child of God.

Chapter 4
Growing Up

Rom 8:30 Moreover whom he did predestinate, them he also called: and whom he called, them he also justified: and whom he justified, them he also glorified.

I remember my mother told me some years back, she had severe complications when she was pregnant and carried me as a foetus, at 7 months, the complications were much that the medical doctor diagnosed the baby as clinically dead, the doctor claimed there was no movement again and some complications and the foetus had died. This has sent shocks to my parents. Though, they were nominal (nominal-they accepted Christianity as a religion, but have not given the Lordship of their lives to Jesus) Christians then, they refuse to give up, took the matter to their shepherd and prayed. According to them, God performed a miracle, the baby resuscitated and kicked, so the attack was overcome.

Then came the time for the naming ceremony, which obviously in this part of Africa; Nigeria precisely, should be a time to celebrate what God has done during the time of carriage and delivery. Alas, the naming ceremony was cancelled; the baby was sick to the point of death and yet again miraculously saved. At some point while I was a child, I have been so much strangely afflicted with sicknesses that defied medical solutions and prescriptions and written off to die by well wishers, but God almighty would always come around to save and heal me. So I grew up getting used to divine intervention and miraculous revival. While it was time for me to walk, I could not walk when other kids walked then and I could not talk when others talked, I stammered. I grew up from so many afflictions from the enemy.

The enemy like He has always done when it is discovered that there is a purpose of God on anyone will always attempt to destroy them to ensure the purpose of God is cut short, also when he knows you have a God-given vision, satan would always try to destroy it at inceptions, satan hates God but he has always failed. satan's style is to try and destroy when they are still young. Let's consider the story of Moses and Jesus as case studies (Exodus 1:16-22 and

> **Exo 1:16 And he said, When ye do the office of a midwife to the Hebrew women, and see *them* upon the stools; if it *be* a son, then ye shall kill him: but if it *be* a daughter, then she shall live.**

> **Exo 1:22 And Pharaoh charged all his people, saying, Every son that is born ye shall cast into the river, and every daughter ye shall save alive.**

> **Mat 2:15 And was there until the death of Herod: that it might be fulfilled which was spoken of the Lord by the prophet, saying, Out of Egypt have I called my son.**

> **Mat 2:16 Then Herod, when he saw that he was mocked of the wise men, was exceeding wroth, and sent forth, and slew all the children that were in Bethlehem, and in all the coasts thereof, from two years old and under, according to the time which he had diligently enquired of the wise men.**

Exactly, when your vision is of God and would impact the kingdom of God, the enemy tries to ensure the atmosphere is not conducive to get it rooted; satan could attack your finances or other things needed just to ensure your vision or dream fail at inception, when it's still very young. The enemy can cause the thrive to drag and attack you multidimensionally, but when you stand and are unshaken, he would leave you for some time and come with strategies as we have seen in the temptation and trial of Jesus.(Luk 4:3-13),the reason believers always need to pray and not faint.

> **Luk 4:13 And when the devil had ended all the temptation, he departed from him for a season.**

I got to know the Lord in 1993 in Osogbo,Osun state, Nigeria under the ministry of Dr. Francis Falola(Manna Bible Church),got baptized in the spirit and water immersion, then I have just finished my secondary school. It is good to know the Lord and the great joy it brought.

Grew up amidst brethren that are fervent, love the Lord and spiritually strong. All my siblings too have given their lives to the Lord and everyone is addicted to Jesus and loves Him. I love evangelism, fasting and prayer.

In 1994, I got admission for my Ordinary National

Diploma at College of Technology, Esa-oke, Osun state, Nigeria to study Civil Engineering, I joined Gospel Students' Fellowship(GSF) at the college, became the bible study teacher and met my wife the following year by divine guidance(I was not praying for a wife, at least to my understanding, yet the Lord said she is my wife, and the Lord had the same time told my wife, though we were not close pals).It was good to see brethren faithfully serving the Lord.

Clothed with Cloud of Glory

God began to manifest His divine presence. In 1995, during my time as a student in school, I have been woken up by the Lord in the midnight around 2am, I have opened my eyes to see smokes beside my bed soaring up, I was scared for I have never had this experience before and I wondered if I have slept outside my room, as I was scared and pondering about this, shining cloud took over my body and covered me like a shining raiment. I have been covered with a cloud like raiment and I could not see my body at all, as this continues, I saw thunderous ligtnings began to blaze in systemic fashions, there was a cooling comfort that took over me. I was afraid and the same time bold not knowing what will happen next. This manifestation was on for some moments and later disappeared. This greatly increased my confidence about divine presence

Psa 8:4 What is man, that thou art mindful of him? and the son of man, that thou visitest him?

Psa 8:5 For thou hast made him a little lower than the angels, and hast crowned him with glory and honour.

In 1998, I have been offered provisional admission to the Polytechnic Ibadan, Oyo state, Nigeria for Higher National Diploma in Civil Engineering. At sango, Ibadan Nigeria, is a church; Scripture Pasture Xtian Centre (outside the school campus). I have been enormously blessed by the Pastor's messages on maturity and perfection. After some time in this church, the Lord spoke to me "feed my sheep, feed my lambs". The Lord asked me to leave the church and proceed into students' fellowship inside the school campus and feed His sheep. It was difficult for me to obey due to personal reasons then. I told the Lord that its difficult since I was relatively unknown to the students' fellowship, gave many reasons to the Lord why I should be left alone. Sometimes our ways are not His ways.

The Lord did not listen to me and He dealt with my health, I became very sickly for I have opened myself to the enemy for refusing the will of God. When we disobey God, we have opened ourselves to the enemy satan.Several days passed and there was no improvement on my health.

> **1Jn 1:9 If we confess our sins, he is faithful and just to forgive us *our* sins, and to cleanse us from all unrighteousness.**

I later asked the Lord for forgiveness on disobedience and promised Him that I would move into the students' fellowship henceforth and that very hour, the sickness left me immediately, the pace of the departure of the sickness was a wonder. So I moved into the students' fellowship based within the campus, and relatively unknown to many of the brethren. I began personal fasting and prayers for days for revival and the release of the anointing of the Holy Spirit upon the fellowship and the brethren. After some time, the Lord during personal prayer and fellowship had called me

President Francis like a friend would call his playmate and some weeks later I became the President of the Fellowship against natural elections.

God has used all these previous assignments, hearing Him and seeing Him fulfill His words as tools to train me for ministry, there is a place of training for efficiency in ministries.

> **Psa 18:34 He *teacheth* my hands to war, so that a bow of steel is broken by mine arms.**

In 1996, I have clearly sensed the calling of God on my life to ministry, I immediately proceeded into 100 days of fasting and prayers to acquire more knowledge about it, and the Lord told me more about it. The burden that consumed my heart was like the ministry would commence the following week. The desire to see it accomplished was great.

I went for my national youth service (NYSC) in 2000 for a compulsory service of my fatherland, Nigeria. I got active secular and career employment in 2003.

Years went by and the burden for ministry gradually declined. I remember in 2009 telling my wife to stop her persistence about answering call to ministry we received some years back. My excuse to her was, Oh! We are trying, we are supporting a local church with our finances and prayers. The secular job has taken hold of me, my time and the best part of me, I was like practically dead to the burden and passion the ministry ought to command in me. It sounded funny, but was real. This is best described as growing cold in the spirit.

For every believer reading this book, there is a call of God on you for ministry. Identify it and fulfill the call of God and as it may apply to you.

Rom 11:29 For the gifts and calling of God *are* without repentance.

2Th 1:11 Wherefore also we pray always for you, that our God would count you worthy of *this* calling, and fulfil all the good pleasure of *his* goodness, and the work of faith with power:

We have been saved as believers and called to fulfill ministry.

Chapter 5
Neglected the Calling, Taken Over by Passion for Career.

Mat 4:18 And Jesus, walking by the sea of Galilee, saw two brethren, Simon called Peter, and Andrew his brother, casting a net into the sea: for they were fishers.

Mat 4:19 And he saith unto them, Follow me, and I will make you fishers of men.

Mat 4:20 And they straightway left *their* nets, and followed him.

My wife had asked me several times before my visit to heaven about my response to the calling of God on my life. My response was very dull and dispassionate .I have been overtaken by love for my job and career. The burden for the calling I once had, had been substituted by career goals alone, this is a clear case of misappropriation.

Unleashing Career Skills, Potentials and Values as Tools for Ministry (Case Studies: Peter and Paul).

David was a shepherd of flocks. God took him from following sheep to be shepherd upon Israel His people. David Knew his credentials or resume, he told Saul and Goliath. Read 1 Samuel 17:1-58.Read what David told Saul

> **1Sa 17:34 And David said unto Saul, Thy servant kept his father's sheep, and there came a lion, and a bear, and took a lamb out of the flock:**

> **1Sa 17:35 And I went out after him, and smote him, and delivered *it* out of his mouth: and when he arose against me, I caught *him* by his beard, and smote him, and slew him.**

> **1Sa 17:36 Thy servant slew both the lion and the bear: and this uncircumcised Philistine shall be as one of them, seeing he hath defied the armies of the living God.**

> **1Sa 17:37 David said moreover, The LORD that delivered me out of the paw of the lion, and out of the paw of the bear, he will deliver me out of the hand of this Philistine. And Saul said unto David, Go, and the LORD be with thee.**

He confronted Goliath with the name of the Lord.

David's experience of God's deliverance so many times have been used as training pitch for him and evidently assisted him when the Lord made him king of Israel.

Some ministries require prior training. No one gets or receives a ministry by accident, if you looked carefully into some ministries/offices , there are evidences or shadows of prior training in time past whether as a servant minister(like Elisha to Elijah) or as a career man/woman(Peter and Paul)

Let's look at the life of Peter

> **Joh 21:3 Simon Peter saith unto them, I go fishing. They say unto him, We also go with thee. They went forth, and entered into a ship immediately; and that night they caught nothing.**

> **Joh 21:6 And he said unto them, Cast the net on the right side of the ship, and ye shall find. They cast therefore, and now they were not able to draw it for the multitude of fishes.**

Peter's ability to wait when there was no fish talked about belief in God to be able to bring forth when the status quo was disturbing. His wait has a similitude to waiting upon God, fasting, prayer for the birth of the will of God, to come forth. Peter's wait before he could get fishes caught and plentiful harvest wherein his nets was torn and was still able to gather the fish to safety is symbolic of five things;

1. Virtues and Characters. Describes Peter as determined, patient, persevering, longsuffering. These virtues are X-rayed in his wait before the turn around. Having a prophetic similitude of the characters expected from those who would be shepherds in the household of God.

2. Prudence to handle surplus when it comes. Peter has mastered prudence from his career.

3. The torn net with the fishes in it, yet carried to safety is symbolic of Peter's ability to demonstrating great skill and confidence in the safety of the church or believers despite tribulation or affliction.

4. Flexible and yielding. Peter's ability to yield to serve God despite Career's prosperities.

5. Humility and obedience. Peter didn't question Jesus's orders despite the fact that Jesus was a total stranger that time. He didn't say, Ah! Who is this Novice teaching a professional?. He simply obeyed

There are success tools/characters that are developed within career ladders .

And Jesus was a carpenter, and with His skills symbolic of his talents in carpentry, He is able to fashion our hearts according to His divine will. He also said I will *build* my church and the gates of hell shall not prevail over it

God has called us to ministry according to the deposits of grace placed on us.

The Combination of Career and Ministry

Joh 21:15 So when they had dined, Jesus saith to Simon Peter, Simon, *son* of Jonas, lovest thou me more than these? He saith unto him, Yea, Lord; thou knowest that I love thee. He saith unto him, Feed my lambs.

Some are called to totally abandon their careers for the ministry, just as it's evident that some folks may not be able to handle ministries together with their careers. There are cases wherein some have turned back to their careers when they are faced with tribulations in their ministries. Therefore some believers will be like Peter who will be called to totally prioritise their careers for the ministry. Jesus said unto Peter, "Loveth thou me more than these?"

> 2Ti 1:9 Who hath saved us, and called *us* with an holy calling, not according to our works, but according to his own purpose and grace, which was given us in Christ Jesus before the world began,

Chapter 6
Every Believer Has a Ministry

What is Ministry? Ministry is an office or a role to which God has called or enabled the saint to function for the edifying or building of the body of Christ.

> **And he gave some, apostles; and some, prophets; and some, evangelists; and some, pastors and teachers; 12 for the perfecting of the saints, for the work of the ministry, for the edifying of the body of Christ: 13 till we all come in the unity of the faith, and of the knowledge of the Son of God, unto a perfect man, unto the measure of the stature of the fullness of Christ: Ephesians 4:11-13**

Apostles, prophets, evangelists, pastors, teachers indicated in vs. 11 are usually been referred to as the 5-fold ministry.

Not every believer would be a pastor or apostle, but every believer has a ministry or calling in the body of Christ. It is the duty of every saint to discover what ministry is to be fulfilled in Christ's vineyard. Your ministry is your God-given area of assignment towards edifying the body. This does not necessarily need to be in the 5-fold.Your reward in heaven is not based on your type of ministry but faithfulness to fulfill or complete. Therefore you need to ask the Lord to tell you which areas of ministry He has for you.

Believers' ministries are to edify the body of Christ. What is your ministry? Pls ask the lord to unveil you. There are many who will discover later on in their days that they have run in vain, that their strengths have been used where it does not matter, it has not benefitted the kingdom. Please do not run in vain, try and discover the will of God for you and how to go about fulfilling your ministry.

Popularity, favours, wealth, though good may not really be the needed signs to show we have performed faithfully or successful in service or ministry, just like a successful church is not in the expanse of crowds. The church today needs to draw a strong divide between what we call success and not. What does it benefit the kingdom for a church ministry described as international with majority of its members wallowing in various forms of sins and same lifestyles with the heathens? All saints will give accounts of their ministries to God.

All saints are stewards, and we would all give accounts of our stewardship.

> Col 4:17 And say to Archippus, Take heed to the ministry which thou hast received in the Lord, that thou fulfil it.

Be Heavenly Minded (The World Is Not Our Place)

> Since you have been raised to new life with Christ, set your sights on the realities of

> heaven, where Christ sits at God's right hand in the place of honor and power. 2 Let heaven fill your thoughts. Do not think only about things down here on earth. 3 For you died when Christ died, and your real life is hidden with Christ in God.Col 3:1-3

Believers need to set their sights and affection firmly on the kingdom of heaven. The realities of heaven according to the above scripture mean heaven is so real that we have to put our gaze firmly, constantly on Christ. Verse 2 says ^Let heaven fill your thoughts. This verse says it all. As believers we would justify our existence in the spirit of power and devotion on earth, when the kingdom of heaven remains our focus. We should stop living like our lives stop here, or like the best part of life is on earth. Heaven is real.

No More Sorrow, No More Pain, No More Crying

> He will remove all of their sorrows, and there will be no more death or sorrow or crying or pain.Rev 21:4.

Heaven- A place of everlasting splendor. There is nothing you could use to describe the eternal bliss with God. For all who have received Jesus into their lives and have lived in accordance to the will and standards of God could be assured an eternity in heaven. Tears, sorrows, death, crying or pain are earthly occurrences, and will not be seen in heaven.

Reader, you must do whatever you could do by giving your life to Jesus Christ and live a life that is pleasing and acceptable to God. You must not miss this.

In my visit to heaven, I discovered that all things work out by the strength of God, I noticed that no matter how long you walk you don't feel pains or tiredness in your legs, and whatever you do you don't feel you have used your strength, there is a power of God divinely that helps you to do whatever you do there so that you don't feel any pains for anything you do at all. Praise God. This is one of the first things I noticed in comparison when I came back to the earth, I noticed I feel tiredness in my legs when I walk for some few meters. I wonder why we struggle and feel the stress to get things done on earth. Heaven is so different to the earth.

Another thing I also want to tell you as emphasized in the above scripture is really no tears. I remember during that period of search for my whereabout in the bush after the robbery attack had ended, the passengers have already called my wife that I could not be found after the robbery attack.

The attack happened around 2am in the midnight, and by 8am, they were still searching for me, so my wife was already crying and praying. I must tell you this as a proof that God hears us so fast when we pray, that the same hour she was crying to the Lord and praying that I should be found from wherever I was hidden. One of the saints in heaven told me someone was looking for me, and at that same time, I saw a woman's face from where I stood, but the face didn't look like my wife or someone I knew, for I had forgotten I was married or had kids, the face looked very bright like an angel with no wrinkle or blemish but part of the face (beneath the eye) was covered with what I could describe as small mask.

I was actually told at two different times by two different saints that someone was looking for me, and at both times I saw the face of this unknown woman, and these were the final stages of my visit and togetherness with saints in heaven, my wife's prayer actually hastened my return to earth so that God could be glorified in all things.

I later realized when I got to earth the meaning of the small mask and the woman's face-The woman's face was actually my wife's face, and the small mask beneath the eye was there because she had cried, and it was covered so that I would not see her tears.

> **He will remove all of their sorrows, and there will be no more death or sorrow or crying or pain. Rev 21:4.**

By 8.45am, my spirit had returned to my body, and the bus passengers could find me.and God made the bus wait till they were able to see me. Praise God!.

Chapter 7
New Bodies Shall Be Given

In heaven, saints have new bodies according to the scriptures. For believers, we can rejoice that we would put on immortality. We would put on new bodies after our earthly experience ends.

Let me remind you that all the people I met in heaven all looked like refreshed young people; they are all putting on new bodies.

> Php 3:20 For our conversation is in heaven; from whence also we look for the Saviour, the Lord Jesus Christ:

> Php 3:21 Who shall change our vile body, that it may be fashioned like unto his glorious body, according to the working whereby he is able even to subdue all things unto himself.

> 1Co 15:44 It is sown a natural body; it is raised a spiritual body. There is a natural body, and there is a spiritual body.

It is necessary to talk again about the saint that showed me his lying-in-state ceremony to illustrate this. I have walked up to him because he smiled at me, he had put out his hand and just immediately we saw the earth, lying-in-state ceremony was going on for him, he was an aged man on earth, he was even fat, placed outside the house. But in heaven he has a slim, youthful body. The bible calls this a spiritual body, fashioned like the Lord's glorious body.

What a privilege to be fashioned in similar bodies like the Lord's.

I want to thank the Lord for bringing me through this to be able to tell my generation.

Chapter 8
The Heavenly Assignment

It has taken me several months to be convinced to write this chapter of my experience in heaven. I have been strengthened to write this phase of my experience particularly knowing my imperfections have been shared too in previous chapters so that no one would unnecessarily think too highly of me as a superhuman. I thank the Lord for the opportunity to reveal what you are going to read now.

Hierarchy in Heaven.

I was led into another apartment inside the house by the particular saint leading me on. This new apartment had very awesome interior decorations, the skating, the floor were very beautiful and lovely to behold. The skating and the floor were the same colour. The previous apartment was very beautiful but the present one has more sophistication.

The apartment also has a book shelf covered up with clouds so I did not identify the titles of the book, there was also a conference table whose face shone forth in a very cool, polished golden colour. I have never seen a place as beautiful as that all my life. At the entrance of the apartment were a white sofa chair and two slim built, elderly looking men seated on it. I was about four to five inches taller than both men, both dressed in white short sleeved raiment.

These men were elders in the house based on the way they have comported themselves; they did not greet me with such pleasantries or flair as I had in the previous apartment. When we came into their apartment, these two men stood up and greeted me like they knew it was their turn to see me.

Comparing both apartment and the saints therein, I could see that there is categorization or classification by ranks in heaven and some are greater than others. Read what Jesus said about the John the Baptist

> **Mat 11:11 Verily I say unto you, among them that are born of women there hath not risen a greater than John the Baptist: notwithstanding he that is least in the kingdom of heaven is greater than he.**

Some people are great in heaven; while some have lesser greatness even their apartments relate this greatness.

The Commissioning, the Sending Forth.

The two elderly saints came forward and with the particular saint leading me on, I was made to stand at the edge of the conference table and there, one of the elderly saints said to me that *"You have not fulfilled your ministry and you have to go back and fulfil your ministry"*, and the elderly saints talked more about the dignity of fulfilling the ministry, their voice tones were gentle and revealed urgencies at the same time.

"Awe" presence all around me as I stood at the other end of the conference table, and the burden for the necessity to depart from the saints and fulfil the ministry came upon me there, the particular saint leading me in the house was so ecstatic with joy that he talked about it too because he saw it and told me some certain things about the ministry too. Thereafter from the apartment, I saw an ash-coloured door before me and I vanished from the house in heaven and this was the time the passengers located me.

I have been sent to proclaim the good tidings and the good news of the Lord Jesus Christ and I am here with the mercies of God to fulfil the mandate.

I thank the Lord for the special opportunity to be able to return back and do His will as He wills according to His plan and purpose for me.

To Him be the Kingdom, the glory and honour, the power and the praise. Amen.

HALLELUJAH BEHOLD HE COMETH SOON.

Christ-The Only
Way to Heaven

I t is my heart desire that you would give your heart to the Lord.

If you would like to receive Jesus into your life, say this prayer

Lord Jesus, I come before you as a sinner, wash my sins by your blood. I believe in my heart and confess with my mouth that Jesus is Lord; I believe Jesus died and rose on the third day for my redemption. I accept Jesus into my heart from today. Write my name into the book of life. Dear Lord, give me grace to live and walk in holiness and purity of lives in Jesus name I pray. Amen.

Congratulations. You are now born again. This simple prayer has opened before you a new course of journey with God. Share your experience with a local church so that you may be encouraged to grow in faith.

Eph 2:19 Now therefore ye are no more strangers and foreigners, but fellowcitizens with the saints, and of the household of God;

Send your testimonies, prayer requests to saintsgather@gmail.com

About the Author

F.O.Owojori is a Telecoms Engineer from Nigeria. He knew the Lord in 1993.Francis has the calling to be a shepherd with a prophetic /apostolic multi-dimensioning. He emphasizes on saints coming to understanding of their roles and responsibilities in the body of Christ and thus are fruitful. Francis has been sent with a clear message to the body of Christ, that the future of Christ's church is likened unto the Living stones' House; 1Peter 2:4-5. He is married and blessed with children